5 Minute Cosy Stories

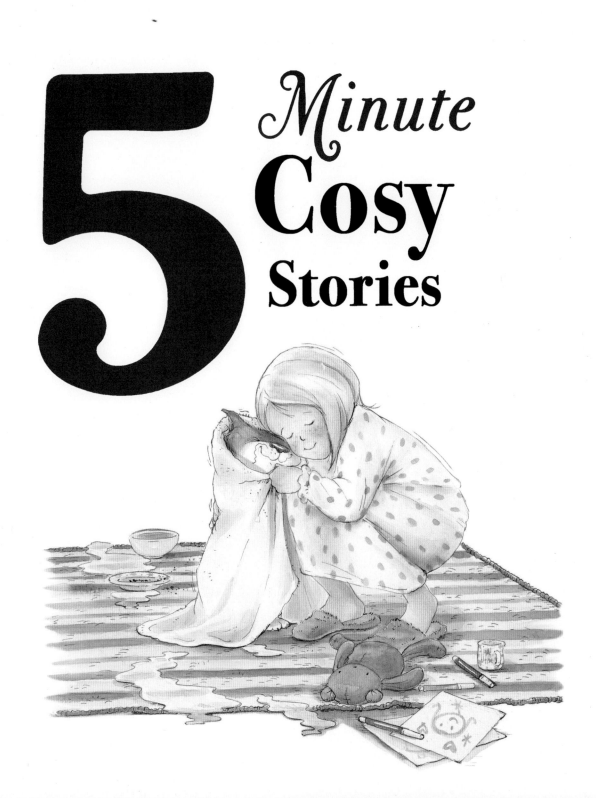

5 Minute Cosy Stories

LITTLE TIGER PRESS
London

Contents

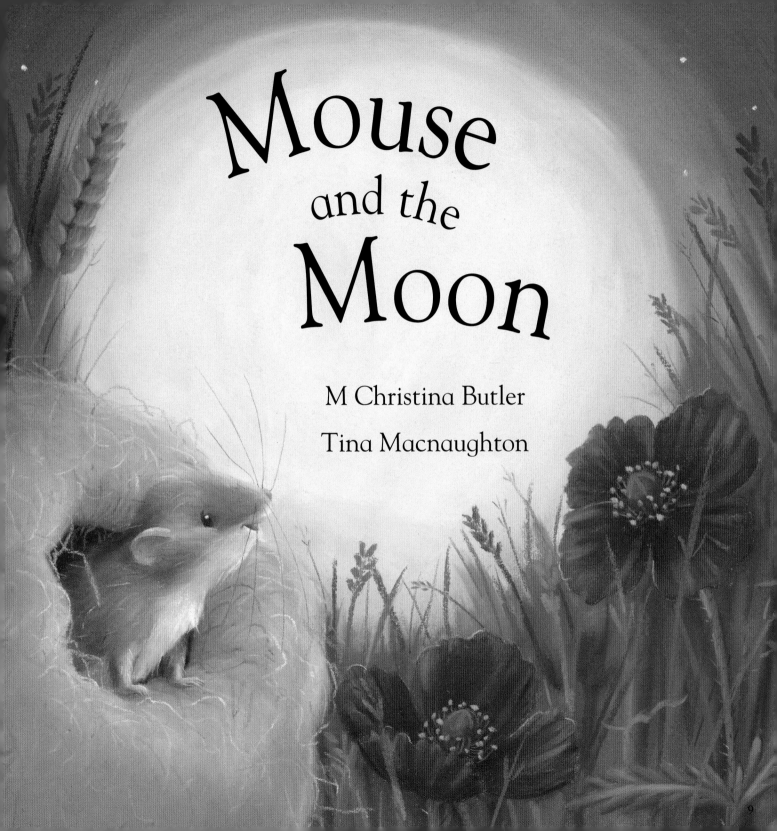

Mouse
and the
Moon

M Christina Butler

Tina Macnaughton

Little Harvest Mouse lived by himself
at the top of the corn. Every night, the
warm summer breezes rocked his cosy
nest, and his friend the moon watched
over him from the deep blue sky.

Before Little Harvest Mouse closed his eyes each night, he sang a lullaby to his very own moon.

But one evening, a cold wind rustled through the corn and Little Harvest Mouse couldn't see his friend anywhere.

Little Harvest Mouse peeked out of his nest.
Everything looked so different without the
moon's friendly glow.

Trembling, he raced through the corn
and across the meadow. "Someone's
stolen the moon!" he shouted
at the top of his voice.

"Stolen the moon?" quacked Duck. "I can't believe
that! The moon will be in the pond where she
always is."

"In the pond?" thought Little Harvest Mouse.
"That can't be!" But he followed Duck as she
looked in the water . . .

The moon was not there.

"Where has she gone?" cried Duck.

"The moon doesn't live in the pond!" laughed Squirrel, who was listening nearby. "She's above my nest in the fir tree."

"The moon doesn't live in a tree!" sniffed Duck.

"She does!" said Squirrel.
He scampered round every branch, but he couldn't find the moon.

"She's not here!" he called down in a panic. "The wind must have blown her away!"

Hare was on his way home when he heard all the fuss.

"Blown the moon away?" he grinned. "Never! She was with me when I ran to the mountains."

"The moon doesn't go to the mountains!" said Squirrel.

"Of course she does!" cried Hare. So they all dashed after him to find the moon.

Little Harvest Mouse searched the sky. Duck looked in every pool and puddle. Squirrel scrambled in and out of the trees, and Hare bounded high and low. But they couldn't find the moon anywhere.

As the wind blew stronger, thunder rumbled round the hills.

"What have you done with my moon, Squirrel?"
snapped Duck.

"It's not your moon, it's mine!" Squirrel cried.
"Anyway, Hare must have lost her!"

"I've done no such thing!" grumbled Hare.

"But what shall I do without her?" squeaked
Little Harvest Mouse. "I'll be all alone!"

FLASH! BOOM! Lightning lit up the sky.
CRACK! CRASH! Thunder clattered
over the mountains.

"Follow me!" shouted Hare. "I know
where there's a cave!"

They
raced
through
the storm
and squeezed
together in
the cave.

"I'm sorry I snapped," whispered Duck.

"It was my fault," Squirrel piped up. "I shouldn't have blamed Hare."

"No harm done," said Hare bravely. And as the storm raged on they told each other stories.

At last, the rain stopped and the clouds rumbled away.

"Look! Look!" cried Little Harvest Mouse.
The clear dark sky was full of twinkling stars,
and peeping out from amongst them was the moon!
It was glowing brightly over the mountains . . .
glittering through the trees . . .
and shining in the pond . . .

"The same moon belongs to us all,"
whispered Duck.
"She never really left us," said Squirrel.
"Good friends never do," nodded Hare wisely.
"And best of all," smiled Little Harvest Mouse,
"she's given me three new friends!"

Newton

Rory Tyger

CREAK, CREAK, CRE-E-EAK!

Newton woke up suddenly. There was a funny noise somewhere in the room.

"Don't be frightened," he told Woffle. "There's always an explanation for everything."

He gave each of his toys a special cuddle so they wouldn't be scared.

CREAK, CREAK, CRE-E-EAK!

went the noise again.

Newton got out of bed and turned on the light.

He walked across the room . . .

"See, toys," he said. "There's nothing to be frightened of. It's only the wardrobe door!"

Newton went back to bed again.

FLAP! FLAP! FLAP!

What was that? Was it a ghost?

Once more Newton got out of bed. He wasn't really scared, but he took his bravest toy, Snappy, just in case. He tiptoed, very quietly, towards the noise.

FLAP! FLAP! FLAP!

it went again. "Of course!" said Newton . . .

"Just what I thought."
It was his bedroom curtains,
flapping in the breeze.
"I'll soon sort those out,"
said Newton.

"You were very brave,
Snappy," he said, as
he closed the window.

SPLISH!

SPLASH!

SPLISH!

Another noise!

Newton looked outside. It wasn't raining.

Besides, the noise wasn't coming from outside.

Nor was it coming from his bedroom. What was it?

"Stay right there, you two," said Newton, "while I look around."

He wasn't the tiniest bit afraid. He was just taking Snappy with him for company.

Newton crept down the corridor. It was
very spooky, especially in the dark corners.

SPLISH! SPLASH! SPLISH!

went the noise.

Very, very quietly, Newton
opened the bathroom door . . .

"Of course, we knew it was the bathroom tap,
didn't we, Snappy," said Newton.

Newton turned off the tap, and
tiptoed back down the corridor.
"Shh," he said to Snappy, just
in case *something* in the dark
corners sprang out at them.

Before he got into bed,
Newton pulled back the
curtains – just to check. It
was very, very quiet outside.

"No more funny noises,"
said Newton.

"You can go to sleep
now," he told all his toys.

RUMBLE! RUMBLE! RUMBLE!

"Oh, no!" cried Newton. "What's that?"

Newton listened very hard. Not a sound.
He was just beginning to think he hadn't
heard anything at all when . . .

RUMBLE! RUMBLE! RUMBLE!

There it was again!

Newton peered under his bed.
Nothing there at all – except for an
old sweet he'd forgotten about.

"Don't worry," said Newton. "We'll
soon find out what it is."

RUMBLE!
Newton stood
very still.

RUMBLE!
Newton listened
very hard.

RUMBLE! went the noise.
And suddenly Newton knew
exactly what it was!

Newton padded downstairs, and into the kitchen.
He helped himself to a large glass of milk and two thick
slices of bread and honey. And now he could hear no

RUMBLE! RUMBLE! RUMBLE!

at all, because . . .

... the rumbling had been
his empty tummy!

Newton went upstairs again, and told his toys
about his rumbling tummy.

"There's always an explanation for everything,"
said Newton, as he climbed back into bed.
"Goodnight, everyone . . ."

"... Sleep tight!"

SNORE, SNORE, SNORE!

went Newton.

I Can Do It!

Tracey Corderoy

Caroline Pedler

Baby Bear had a new rucksack.
It was *brilliant*, but the big green
button was tricky for little paws!
   All morning, Baby Bear tried
and tried to open and close it.

"Mummy! Look!"
he cried at last.

"I can do it!"

"Clever you!" Mummy said. "Why don't we pop some books in to take back to the library?"

"I can do it!" Baby Bear smiled. And he squeezed *all* the books into his rucksack. Every one!

But it was just a
bit too heavy . . .

Ooops!

Mummy took a few books
out to carry then tried to
help with his coat.
"No, I can do it!"
Baby Bear said.
He wriggled into
it and did up *all*
the buttons!

"Come on,
Barnaby," he said
to his toy bunny.
"Let's go!"

71

Baby Bear skipped into town
and stopped at the crossing.
"I can press the button!"
he said.
But somebody *else*
pressed it first . . .

"I wanted to do it!" Baby Bear grumbled.

And he plodded on sadly with Mummy.

At the library, Baby Bear raced off to find
Barnaby's favourite bunny book. But it
was up **very** high.

"Don't worry, Barnaby," Baby Bear said.
"I'll get it!"

He stood on tippy-toes,
but he couldn't reach.

He hopped and he jumped,
but he *still* couldn't reach.

"Oh, bother!" said Baby Bear.
He really wanted to get the
book *all by himself.*

So Baby Bear built a big tower of cushions, and clambered right to the top.
    But suddenly the tower started to sway . . .

Wibble!

Wobble!

"Oh no!" cried Baby Bear.

And
down he
tumbled . . .

79

...bump!

"Mummy!" he howled, and
Mummy rushed over.

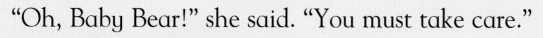

"Oh, Baby Bear!" she said. "You must take care."

"I couldn't reach the story," sniffed Baby Bear.

Mummy gave him a big hug. "You can
do *lots* of things by yourself,
but when things are a bit
too tricky you just need
to ask for help."

"OK," Baby Bear nodded.

Mummy helped reach down the story.
Baby Bear and Barnaby then turned the
pages and Mummy read the words.
Sometimes having a little bit
of help was fine.

When it was time to go,
Baby Bear packed
his rucksack all
by himself.

Then he helped Mummy
with her coat.
  "I can do it!"
Baby Bear said . . .

"Thank you, Baby Bear!"
smiled Mummy.
   Then Baby Bear skipped
off home, singing . . .

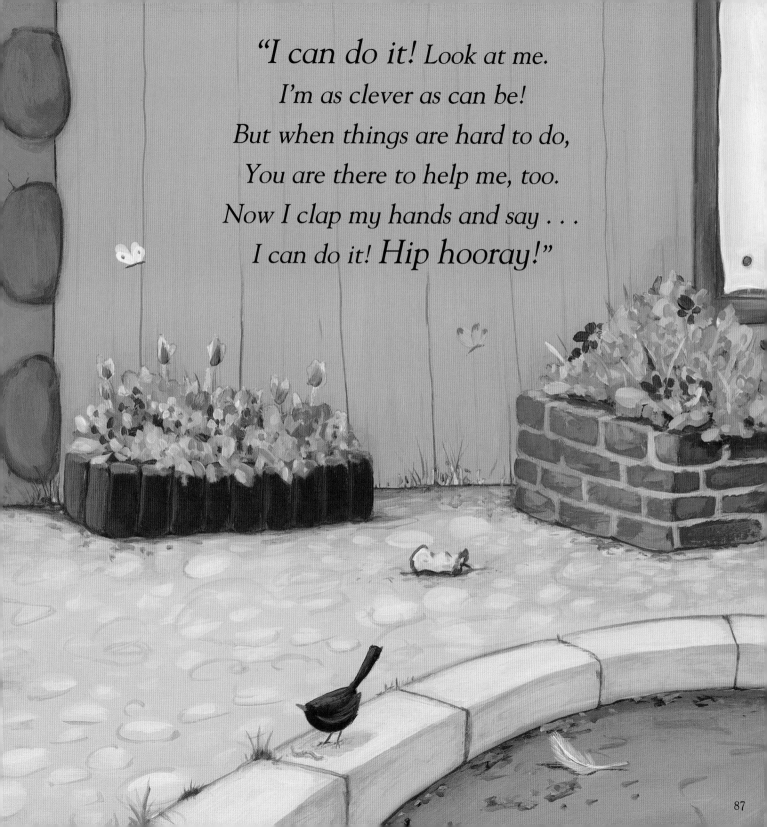

"*I can do it! Look at me.*
I'm as clever as can be!
But when things are hard to do,
You are there to help me, too.
Now I clap my hands and say . . .
I can do it! Hip hooray!"

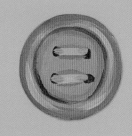

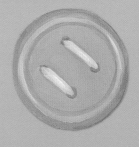

The Most Precious Thing

Gill Lewis

Louise Ho

Little Bear was taking Mummy Bear on
a walk through the forest in the autumn
sunlight. She wanted to show her the
special place where the juiciest berries
and the sweetest nuts could be found.

As Little Bear skipped through
the rustling leaves, she suddenly
spied a small blue stone glittering
in the sunshine.

"Look, Mummy, look!" cried Little Bear, picking
it up. "Look at this shiny jewel I have found."
Little Bear gazed as it sparkled in her paw.
"It must be the most precious thing in the whole
wide world," she gasped.

"Oh yes, Little
Bear, this is a very
beautiful stone," said
Mummy Bear, holding it up
so that it twinkled in the light,
"but the most precious thing is
even prettier than this."

"Really?" said Little Bear in wonder. She
put the stone carefully in her bag. "Let's go
and look! I want to find the most precious
thing EVER!"

"Wait for me," laughed Mummy Bear, as
Little Bear scampered off through the trees.

Little Bear and Mummy Bear played games in the afternoon sun. They tried to catch the seeds that spun in the breeze. And Little Bear kept looking for something prettier than the little blue stone.

After a while they came to Little Bear's
special place and they filled their tummies
with juicy purple blackberries.
Little Bear was reaching
for a berry when she saw
something pink hidden
in the brambles . . .

It was a beautiful wild rose.

"Mummy!" shouted Little
Bear excitedly. "Come and
see what I have found!"

She stroked the rose's silky
petals and sniffed its sweet smell.
"I've never seen such a pretty
flower. Surely this must be the
most precious thing?"

"This rose is very pretty, Little Bear," said Mummy Bear, "and it's soft as velvet." She tickled the rose against Little Bear's nose, making her sneeze. "But the most precious thing is even softer than this."

Little Bear wondered what on earth could be
softer than her beautiful rose. She searched and
searched through the dry, crunchy leaves, but
she found only spiky horse chestnuts,
bristly pine cones and a
rather cross hedgehog!

Just then she caught sight of something fluttering
high up in the trees.

"Look up there!" she shouted. "That *has* to be it!"

Mummy Bear lifted Little Bear up into the air. Caught in a spider's web was a tiny fluffy feather. Little Bear reached up high and took the feather very gently in her paw.

Little Bear touched the downy feather against her cheek.

"Oh Mummy," she whispered hopefully. "Please tell me. Is this the most precious thing?"

"It is very soft," said Mummy Bear, "but the most precious thing is even better than this – it makes me want to dance for joy."

And Mummy Bear twirled Little Bear round, making her giggle.

Little Bear was determined to find the most precious thing. She ran up a grassy hilltop to look out at the woods and fields. Hundreds of dazzling butterflies suddenly filled the air around her.

One of the butterflies landed lightly on her paw. Little Bear gazed at it in wonder.

"This is it!" she sang out happily. "At last I have found the most precious thing in the whole of the big wide world."

Little Bear and Mummy Bear lay in the long grass as the butterfly fluttered through the golden sunlight.

"Oh yes, that is very special," said Mummy Bear softly, "but I can hold the most precious thing safe and tight in my arms."

"Oh, please tell me what it is!" said Little Bear crossly. "I have looked absolutely everywhere and I still haven't found it."

Mummy Bear smiled. "The most precious thing is prettier than any jewel, is softer than a rose or the fluffiest feather, and fills me with more joy than a dancing butterfly. The most precious thing . . ." she said, hugging Little Bear tightly, ". . . is you!"

The
Wish
Cat

Ragnhild Scamell

Gaby Hansen

Holly's house had a cat flap.
It was a small door in the
big door so a cat could come
and go.

　　But Holly didn't have a cat.

One night, something magical happened. Holly saw a falling star.

As the star trailed across the sky, she made a wish.

"I wish I had a kitten," she whispered. "A tiny cuddly kitten who could jump in and out of the cat flap."

CRASH!

Something big landed on the window sill outside.
It wasn't a kitten . . .

It was Tom, the scruffiest, most raggedy cat
Holly had ever seen. He sat there in the
moonlight, smiling a crooked smile.

"Miao-o-ow!"

"I'm Tom, your wish cat," he seemed to say.

"It's a mistake," cried Holly.
"I wished for a kitten."

Tom didn't think Holly had
made a mistake.

126

He rubbed his torn ear
against the window and
howled so loudly it made
him cough and splutter.

"Miao-o-ow, o-o-w, o-o-w!"

Holly hid under her
duvet, hoping that
he'd go away.

The next morning, Tom was still there, waiting for her outside the cat flap. He wanted to come in, and he had brought her a present of a smelly old piece of fish.

"Yuk!" said Holly. She picked
it up and dropped it in the
dustbin. Tom looked puzzled.
"Bad cat," she said, shooing
him away.

"Go on, go home!" said
Holly, walking across
to her swing.

129

But Tom was there before her. He sharpened his claws on the swing . . .

and washed his coat noisily, pulling out bits of fur and spitting them everywhere.

At lunchtime, Tom sat on the
window sill, watching Holly eat.

She broke off a piece of her sandwich and
passed it out to him through the cat flap.
Tom wolfed it down, purring all the while.

In the afternoon, a cold wind swept through the garden, and Holly had to wear her jacket and scarf. Tom didn't seem to feel the cold. He followed her around . . .

chasing leaves . . .

balancing along the
top of the fence . . .

showing off.

Soon it was time for Holly
to go indoors to tea.

"Bye then, Tom," she said,
and stroked his tatty
head.

Tom followed her across to the door
and settled himself by the cat flap.

That evening, it snowed.
Gleaming pompoms of
snow danced in the air.

Outside the cat flap,
Tom curled himself into a
ragged ball to keep warm.
Soon there was a white
cushion of snow all over
the doorstep, and on Tom.

Holly heard him miaowing miserably.
She ran to the cat flap and held it open . . .

Tom came in, shaking snow all over
the kitchen floor.

"Poor old Tom," said Holly.

He ate a large plate of food, and drank
an even larger bowl of warm milk.

Tom purred louder than ever when
Holly dried him with the kitchen towel.

Soon Tom had settled down, snug on Holly's bed.

Holly stroked his scruffy fur, and together they watched the glittering stars.

Then, suddenly, another star fell. Holly couldn't think of a single thing to wish for. She had everything she wanted. And so had Tom.

145

I Love You More Each Day!

Suzanne Chiew   Tina Macnaughton

You're my sunshine, little one,
You are the world to me.

You find such joy and wonder
In everything you see.

I love each happy thing you do,
Each funny thing you say.
From spring to summer, all year through,
I love you more each day.

Each day is bright
and beautiful,
Each day holds
something new . . .

153

And every day is magical
When it is shared with you.

I love the gifts you give me
And the silly games we play.
Your smiles and giggles warm my heart –
More than words can say.

When summer comes
we splish and splash
In oceans deep and blue.

You show me hidden treasures,
But none so sweet as you.

Each kind and gentle thing you do,
Each thoughtful thing you say,
Makes me so very proud of you.
I love you more each day.

Whether we're
still and quiet,
Watching rainbows
paint the sky . . .

Or whether we're
loud and playful,
Tossing fallen
leaves up high . . .

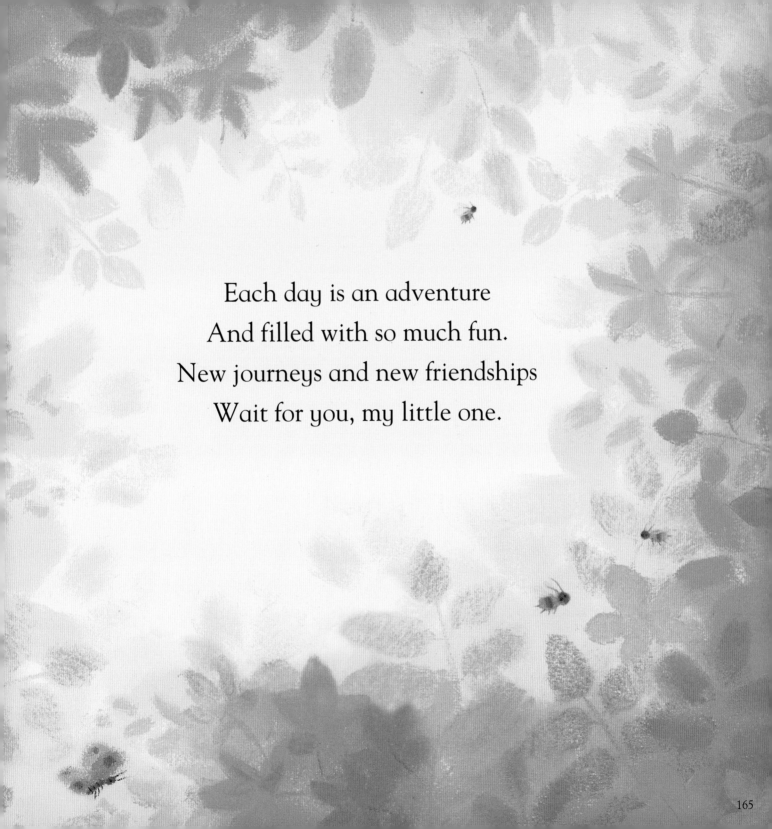

Each day is an adventure
And filled with so much fun.
New journeys and new friendships
Wait for you, my little one.

You love to stomp
through snowdrifts
As our world turns
sparkly white . . .

And find each pretty, frosted leaf
That twinkles in the light.

Although the seasons turn and change,
Our love will always stay
From springtime through to winter,
I love you more each day.

When sparkling stars shine brightly,
We snuggle up together.
I love you more and more each day,
And more and more for ever!

172

Have You Got My Purr?

Judy West   Tim Warnes

"Oh Mummy, Mummy!"

"What's the matter, little Kitten?

Why are you crying?"

"Oh Mummy, Mummy, I've lost my purr."

"You'll find your purr, little Kitten.

Just wait and see."

177

"Oh Dog, Dog, have you got my purr?"

"Woof, woof," said Dog, licking his bone.

"I haven't got your purr, little Kitten.

This is my *woof*. Why don't you ask Cow?"

"Oh Cow, Cow, have
you got my purr?"
"Moo, moo," said Cow,
flicking flies with
her ears.

MOO

MOO

"I haven't got your purr,
little Kitten. This is my *moo*.
Why don't you ask Pig?"

"Oh Pig, Pig, have you got my purr?"
  "Oink, oink," said Pig, snuffling
in the straw.

"Oh Duck, Duck, have you
got my purr?"
   "Quack, quack," said Duck,
splashing in the water.

"I haven't got your purr, little Kitten. This is my *quack*. Why don't you ask Mouse?"

185

"Oh Mouse, Mouse, have you got my purr?"
"Squeak, squeak," said Mouse, nibbling cheese
in the barn. "I haven't got your purr, little Kitten.
This is my *squeak*. Why don't you ask Sheep?"

SQUEAK SQUEAK

"Oh Sheep, Sheep, have you got my purr?"
"Baa, baa," said Sheep, munching grass in
the field. "I haven't got your purr, little Kitten.
This is my *baa*. Why don't you ask wise old Owl?"

189

"Wise old Owl, have you
got my purr?"
"Hoot, hoot," said the wise
old Owl, blinking his
big round eyes.

HOOT
HOOT

"I haven't got your purr, little Kitten.
This is my *hoot*. Why don't you go
back and ask your mother?"

"Oh Mummy, Mummy," wailed little Kitten. "*Nobody's* got my purr. Dog hasn't got it. He's got a woof. Cow hasn't got it. She's got a moo. Pig hasn't got it. She's got an oink. Duck hasn't got it. She's got a quack. Mouse hasn't got it. He's got a squeak. Sheep hasn't got it. She's got a baa. Wise old Owl hasn't got it. He's got a hoot. Oh Mummy, Mummy, I've lost my purr!"

"You haven't lost your purr,
little Kitten. Come here
and I'll explain."

"Nobody's got your purr.
Your purr is inside you
when you're happy!
Listen, little Kitten,
listen . . ."

"My *purr*!
Oh, Mummy.
I've found my purr!
It was here
all the time."
    So little Kitten
curled up . . .

and purred and purred
and purred.

PURR PURR

When We're Together

Claire Freedman   Jane Chapman

Together is waking to bright summer sunshine,
With happy songs filling your head,
It's singing the words at the top of your voice
As you bounce up and down on your bed.

Being together is running down hillsides,
So fast that you almost can't stop!
Together is landing in one giant heap,
And catching your breath as you flop.

Together's the fun that you have when it's snowing,
The sledges you can't wait to ride,
It's giggling while trying to hold up each other
Whenever your feet slip and slide!

Being together is having a secret
You share with your very best friend,
It's talking and listening and laughing together,
And knowing your friendship won't end.

Time spent together is getting all messy,
It's squidgy mud pies that you pat,
It's squashing and squelching
and stamping them down,
And hearing the sound as they splat!

213

Together is riding on Daddy's
strong shoulders,
And feeling as tall as a tree,
It's going exploring and having adventures,
And sharing new things that you see.

Together is kicking through leaves,
crisp and crunchy,
And watching them swirl through the air,
It's leaping in drifts that come up to your knees,
And showering the leaves everywhere.

Being together is fireside cuddles,
It's magical stories we share,
It's hearing the rain pitter-pat on the windows,
Squish-squashed in our favourite chair.

Together is searching in seaweedy rock pools,
Then catching a crab in your hand,
It's squealing as cold waves rush over your feet,
And wiggling your toes in the sand.

Sometimes together is just being quiet,
Like gazing at clouds in the sky,
It's seeing the shapes and the patterns they make,
And counting them as they float by.

Together is pillow fights all round your bedroom,
And giggling and running to hide,
It's white fluffy feathers that fly through the air
So it looks like it's snowing inside.

Time spent together is big hugs at bedtime,
And being tucked in snug and tight,
It's sweet dreams and moonbeams
and drowsy eyes closing,
And sleeping safe all through the night.

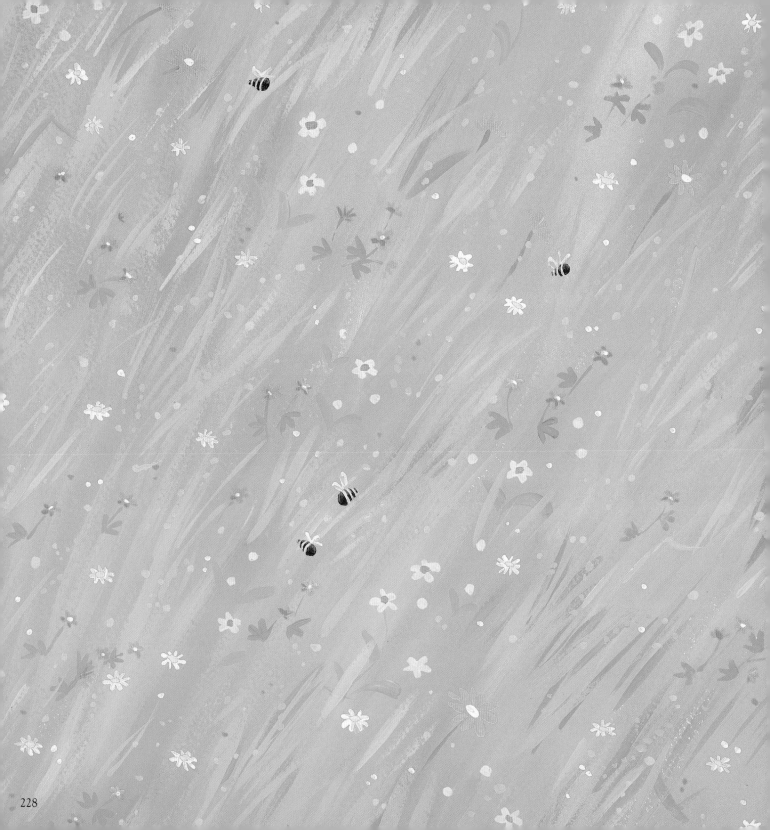

5 MINUTE COSY STORIES

LITTLE TIGER PRESS
1 The Coda Centre,
189 Munster Road,
London SW6 6AW
www.littletiger.co.uk

First published in Great Britain 2016

Printed in China • LTP/1800/1524/0516

ISBN 978-1-84869-334-0

2 4 6 8 10 9 7 5 3 1

231

THE WISH CAT

Ragnhild Scamell
Illustrated by Gaby Hansen

First published in Great Britain 2001
by Little Tiger Press

I LOVE YOU MORE EACH DAY!

Suzanne Chiew
Illustrated by Tina Macnaughton

First published in Great Britain 2013
by Little Tiger Press

HAVE YOU GOT MY PURR?

Judy West
Illustrated by Tim Warnes

First published in Great Britain 1999
by Little Tiger Press

WHEN WE'RE TOGETHER

Claire Freedman
Illustrated by Jane Chapman

First published in Great Britain 2009
by Little Tiger Press